BREEDING COCKATIELS
KW-099

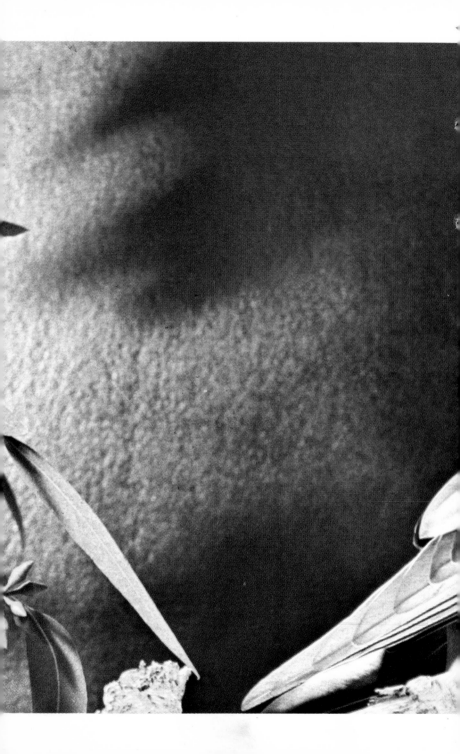

Contents

Photographers: Dr. Gerald R. Allen, Glen S. Axelrod, Dr. Herbert R. Axelrod, H. Bielfeld, Isabelle Francais, Michael Gilroy, E. Goldfinger, Jack Harris, B. Kahl, Bruce D. Lavoy, N. Richmond, Brian Seed, Vince Serbin, Julie Sturman, Dr. Martin F. Sturman, Vogelpark Walsrode.

Endpapers: A young adult cockatiel. Photo courtesy of the San Diego Zoo. **Title page:** Headstudy of a normal gray cockatiel.

Distributed in the UNITED STATES by T.F.H. Publications, Inc., One T.F.H. Plaza, Neptune City, NJ 07753; in CANADA to the Pet Trade by H & L Pet Supplies Inc., 27 Kingston Crescent, Kitchener, Ontario N2B 2T6; Rolf C. Hagen Ltd., 3225 Sartelon Street, Montreal 382 Quebec; in CANADA to the Book Trade by Macmillan of Canada (A Division of Canada Publishing Corporation), 164 Commander Boulevard, Agincourt, Ontario M1S 3C7; in ENGLAND by T.F.H. Publications Limited, Cliveden House/Priors Way/Bray, Maidenhead, Berkshire SL6 2HP, England; in AUSTRALIA AND THE SOUTH PACIFIC by T.F.H. (Australia) Pty. Ltd., Box 149, Brookvale 2100 N.S.W., Australia; in NEW ZEALAND by Ross Haines & Son, Ltd., 18 Monmouth Street, Grey Lynn, Auckland 2, New Zealand; in SINGAPORE AND MALAYSIA by MPH Distributors (S) Pte., Ltd., 601 Sims Drive, #03/07/21, Singapore 1438; in the PHILIPPINES by Bio-Research, 5 Lippay Street, San Lorenzo Village, Makati Rizal; in SOUTH AFRICA by Multipet Pty. Ltd., 30 Turners Avenue, Durban 4001. Published by T.F.H. Publications, Inc. Manufactured in the United States of America by T.F.H. Publications, Inc.

BREEDING COCKATIELS

JULIE STURMAN WITH DOROTHY SCHULTS

Above: *Co-author Julie Sturman with her champion Labrador Retriever and another of her psittacine friends, a blue-crowned Amazon parrot.* **Opposite:** *An albino cockatiel with very red eyes.*

Getting Started

Of all the small pet birds, cockatiels are our favorites, and most breeders will agree they are by far the easiest to breed. For the most part, they are friendly to people and to other birds, and your pet bird should accept a newcomer with relative ease. Cockatiels are usually strong and healthy. Their colorful plumage, charming personalities and adaptability make them most desirable as pets and excellent birds for novice breeders. Furthermore, they are easily acquired, there is a selection of color, the sexes can usually be differentiated without too much difficulty and—most important— they are very easy to breed in captivity.

While several other species of small cage birds require the presence of three or four other pairs in order to settle into breeding, a single pair of cockatiels should produce for you within a short time. These delightful little birds are usually excellent parents who will rear their chicks with little or no extra help. We will discuss at length many of the difficult situations that may by chance occur, but it should be stressed at the outset that nature is on your side. We know that often the hardest thing to do is nothing, and the urge to help is understandable. The information in this book will show you what to expect and how to tell when your assistance may be

necessary as well as when to let your birds alone and simply watch what happens.

We hope you will have much pleasure and success breeding cockatiels for the first time, and, since no two pairs are exactly alike, we expect you will use *Breeding Cockatiels* as a handy and useful reference for your future breedings as well.

SELECTING THE BIRDS

If you already have one cockatiel, you can buy another of the opposite sex and bring it home to launch your breeding activities. One of our very tame pairs seemed happy to be handled all through the mating and laying period and even after the chicks were hatched. This behavior is somewhat unusual, though. Many times, a parent cockatiel—the male bird especially—will become protective and develop a tendency to bite in an attempt to keep you away from its mate. You must recognize that while it is perfectly acceptable to breed your pet, once it has a mate the birds will be far more interested in each other than they are in you. If your pet cockatiel is exceptionally tame and you spend hours playing and

Opposite: *The cockatiel is a hardy and healthy little bird which is simple to keep and easy to breed. As it is relatively easy to differentiate the sexes, selecting a breeding pair should not be difficult, even for the novice.*

Above: *A compatible pair of cockatiels, a gray normal male and a pearlie female.*
Opposite: *A pair of adult cinnamons.*

talking with it, it might be better to keep it as your pet and buy a breeding pair.

Whether you are buying one bird or two, be sure to go to a reputable dealer. Successful breeding begins with healthy birds. Healthy cockatiels have clear, very bright eyes that literally sparkle. Be sure to check their droppings too. The droppings should be well formed and not runny. Feathers should have a glossy sheen, and the birds should have a sleek look.

Most untrained cockatiels shiver and shake when they are nervous or when they're being closely watched. This is not an indication of poor health; it may only be an indication that the birds have had little human contact. However, if a bird sits still, puffs up and looks drowsy, it may be ill. You should know, though, that young birds require a lot of rest. They nap frequently, and at certain times a puffed-up appearance, closed eyes and a tired look are perfectly normal. Morning or early evening hours are the best times for selection. The birds are usually hungry and alert upon awakening and again late in the afternoon or early evening.

If you are buying primarily for breeding purposes, try to purchase older birds. There will then be no doubt as to their sex and maturity. Sometimes, breeders will sell a proven breeding pair. In order to be considered proven, the birds must have mated, produced eggs, hatched live chicks and (preferably) raised them successfully. If you get such a pair, you have the advantage of knowing the birds are compatible and not sterile. Though it happens infrequently, some birds, especially white males, may be sterile, so we recommend that your first attempts at breeding not be done with a white male unless he has been proven.

If you do purchase a proven pair, try to ascertain that they have not been overbred. Overbred birds, especially the hens, have a haggard, burnt-out look. Birds that are permitted to produce over and over again without several months of rest may produce inferior chicks. Cockatiels are not unique; like other animals, they need to have time to restore themselves to top physical condition before going through the strenuous breeding cycle.

COLOR

The most common cockatiel color is gray. Gray is the basic color of wild cockatiels, so it is called the normal cockatiel color. Males have well-defined markings. Their faces are vivid yellow with clear, bright, circular patches of orange on their cheeks. They have a striking border of white feathers along the shoulder edges of their wings, and their underwings and tail feathers are a

Cockatiels are friendly birds; therefore, the breeder should have little trouble in finding a compatible mate for his bird.

solid darker gray. Normal females have a subdued version of the same markings. Yellow, if any, is sparse and dull, and their orange cheek patches are somewhat indistinct. If you spread their wings and look at the undersides, you will see striping or bars across the feathers. The same bars will be observed on the undersides of the long tail feathers.

White cockatiels can be snowy white or may have a pale yellow cast. They have the same bright yellow heads and the bright orange cheek patches as the normals, or grays. Males and females in the white variety are almost identical, although the female's markings may be slightly paler. Like the gray hens, white females also have striping under their wings and tails, but this striping is usually pale yellow and much more difficult to discern. If you hold the spread wings up to a strong light, faint markings will definitely be present in female white birds. White birds may have dark eyes or red eyes. The red-eyed birds are not true albinos, since they have color in their feathers. There is much controversy about the proper name for these birds. Some fanciers call them albinos,

Above: *A normal gray male on a perch that is too small in diameter.* **Opposite:** *Note the alert look of this healthy young cockatiel. Young birds should be aware of and interested in their surroundings.*

whereas other fanciers call them lutinos or simply whites. It is inadvisable to breed two red-eyed whites together, because their offspring are subject to eye weakness and possible blindness.

Pied cockatiels are a variegation of grays and whites. Their harlequin markings may be heavy or light. White pieds have splashes of gray, and (more commonly) gray pieds have splashes of white and yellow. Males, if predominantly gray, will display the vivid yellow and orange facial markings. Otherwise the sexes are similar in color. No two pied birds are marked exactly alike. Symmetrical markings are the most desirable.

Pearlies, also called opalines, are most interesting. Though both sexes are heavily marked, only the females retain their markings at maturity. After the first molt, males revert to the typical gray coloration. It is hoped that eventually a strain will be developed in which pearlie males keep their decorative plumage to maturity. At the present time, we know of no such strain. Pearlies have gray feathers heavily tipped with yellow and white, giving an all-over pleasing speckled effect. They too have more yellow around the head and they have orange cheeks.

Cinnamons are a relatively recent mutation of gray. They are actually a pale cinnamon color which many times looks like a washed-out gray. The deeper brownish tones are desirable. Cinnamons are becoming more popular and are less difficult to obtain than they have been in the past.

There are many breeders experimenting and developing new mutations all the time, so you may hear of some we didn't mention. These five, though, are the colors you are most likely to find when you go shopping for your cockatiels.

Genetics for color breeding could fill another book, and since in most cases you won't know your bird's ancestry, it is not necessary that you study all the possible combinations and probable outcomes. Without knowing your bird's background, it is extremely difficult to predict what color the chicks will be—besides, it's exciting to watch the chicks develop their color. As a general rule, breeding gray to gray will produce gray chicks. If you have a split gray (that is, one with white or pied in its background), it will have a small patch of white in the neck region. These splits can produce white or pied offspring. Breeding white to white will most likely produce nothing but white chicks. Just remember that at least one white parent should be dark-eyed. White cockatiels have a tendency for baldness on their heads. This is another thing you may not wish to perpetuate.

We set up three pairs for

A cageful of cockatiels and parrots. Although cockatiels are usually friendly with other species, it is wise to house cockatiels with cockatiels only.

breeding recently. One was a split gray male with a pearlie hen, one pair was a gray male with a white hen and the third pair was two pieds. The possibilities are almost endless, so pick birds whose colors appeal to you and see what you get.

DETERMINING SEXES

It is difficult to determine the sex of very young birds. At first, both sexes look like females, but the brilliant colors of the male intensify with maturity. Some breeders use a trick to speed up nature a little. Pluck one tail feather from a young cockatiel. Within two weeks a new feather will begin to grow. If it is solid in color, the bird is a male. If the new feather has even faint stripes or bars when held up to a strong light, the bird is a female. When the birds are past six months of age and their color is in, the grays and pieds are fairly

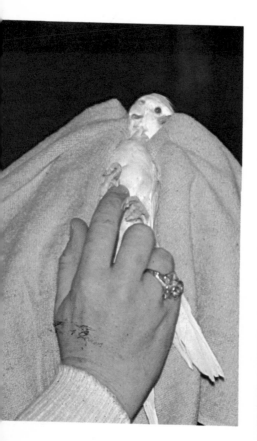

Above left: *A demonstration of how to sex a cockatiel.* **Above right:** *A pied male cockatiel.* **Opposite:** *A beautiful opaline cockatiel.*

easy to sex by observing their facial markings. Pearlie males lose their markings with maturity, so a pearlie-marked bird over a year old is a female. Since white males and females look alike, only by comparing many of them will you be able to notice deeper coloration on the facial markings of the males. For white birds, then, other means of determining sex are necessary.

As previously mentioned, females of all colors have bars or stripes, no matter how faintly colored, on the undersides of their wings and tails. Males do not.

If you turn your birds upside down and place your finger over the vent, you will feel two bony ridges. In the male they are very close together. Females have a wider space between the ridges and have a feel of flexibility. Again, comparison will be necessary for positive identification.

EQUIPMENT FOR BREEDING

You can use the bird cage you already have, providing it is large enough to comfortably accommodate two cockatiels and has room for an additional perch so that the chicks have a place to sit when they emerge from the nest. You will need a nesting box. Good boxes are usually available at well-stocked pet shops and are so inexpensive it doesn't pay to make your own. However, if you are so inclined, these boxes are

simply constructed from lightweight plywood and are easily put together. A typical cockatiel nesting box is about twelve inches square with a round opening in the front about three inches in diameter so the birds can move freely in and out. There is a perch under this round opening that extends about three to four inches inside the box and about three to four inches on the outside. Most nesting boxes have a sliding panel in the back or on the side so you can open the box without disturbing it to see what's going on inside. Birds will sit on the perch at the entrance to their nest looking in from outside or out from inside.

With a pair of wire clippers, you can remove about three rungs from the side or back of your cage and attach the nesting box to the outside of the cage with small metal hooks and eyes. Place the box so that the hole you made in your cage corresponds to the entrance to the nest. After your chicks are out of the nest, your cage can easily be repaired with wire from a coat hanger or by covering the hole with a thin sheet of metal. There is no need for the hobby breeder who is breeding only one pair of cockatiels for fun to invest in a lot of expensive equipment. There will be plenty of time for that later on should you decide to expand your aviary.

Before you hang your nesting box, it is very important to spray it thoroughly with a good bird insecticide. Even if you buy a brand-new box, it may have been stored near birds infested with mites and may be harboring a family of these pests. A thorough spraying and even a scalding with boiling water is an easy precaution and one you will not regret having taken. Be sure you get into the cracks, corners and crevices in the wood with the spray or hot water. If you elect to scrub the box be sure the wood is thoroughly dry before you offer the box to your birds.

Cockatiels do enjoy baths and will often bathe in their water cups if there is room. Therefore, be sure to provide tepid water, not cold, especially in the winter. Change the water frequently, at least twice a day, to be sure it is fresh and clean at all times. In order to avoid having the birds soil their drinking water by bathing in it, you might want to install in the cage a hanging water bottle such as those used for hamsters, mice and other small caged animals. If you do this, be sure your cockatiels know how to use it before you remove all other drinking water from their cage.

A small pottery dish or shallow bowl, heavy enough to be tip-proof when a cockatiel perches on its edge, may be placed in the cage daily for bathing. Always offer the bath before noon to allow the birds ample drying time before evening. The bathing habit should be encouraged, as the moisture will

A trio of cockatiels on a nesting box. When setting up a breeding area, be sure to provide enough boxes for all pairs. In addition, be sure to remove all unpaired birds from the breeding area.

aid in preventing egg shells from becoming hard and brittle. It will help to prevent egg breakage and will facilitate hatching too.

If the birds refuse to bathe, spray them with a fine mist of lukewarm (not hot or cold) water daily. They will soon learn to enjoy these water sports and will look

Opposite: *A pair of cockatiels chewing on a cuttlebone. Cuttlebone is a necessity for healthy cockatiels, especially during the breeding season.* **Above:** *"Chica Schults," one of the authors' cockatiels.*

forward to them each morning. In cold weather, it might be wise to limit bathing to two or three times a week. There is no problem, though, in a comfortably warm home.

Another piece of equipment that can be very helpful is a small long-handled net for catching the birds should they escape from their cage. If you should have to transfer them from one cage to another, or should they by chance get out while you are cleaning the cage or adding food or water, chasing them wildly while they are flying around the house can cause untamed birds to panic and possibly injure themselves. If you wait for the birds to settle on a window ledge or piece of furniture and then approach them quietly

A breeding pair of cockatiels will become more interested in each other than in their owner. The attention they pay to each other is a good sign that a clutch of eggs is soon to follow.

Cage toys are wonderful diversions for the pet cockatiel, but the breeding cockatiel can do without them. Indeed, the cockatiel breeder would be wise to save room for the nest box and some perches.

with a net, your job will be made much easier and the birds will be caused much less anxiety.

In addition, get a few small plastic eyedroppers for administering medication should it be necessary, a pair of nail clippers and a smaller net that will fit through the opening of the cage.

Above: *Two views of a female exhibiting typical wild coloration.* **Below:** *Two views of a typical pied cockatiel.*

Above: *Two views of a male exhibiting typical wild coloration.* **Below:** *Front and rear views of a nice pearl cockatiel.*

Breeding

Now your nesting box is ready and hung onto the cage. You have a compatible pair of cockatiels and you are ready to become a breeder. The diet of your potential breeders will be an important factor affecting your success in breeding cockatiels, so we'll now make specific recommendations about a feeding regimen that has worked well for us. If your cockatiels are maintained on a rich, well-balanced diet, there is no need to change or supplement it during breeding. As a matter of fact, change at that time can be detrimental. If the hen reacts to a new food with diarrhea, she is likely to abandon her eggs and you will have no chicks.

DIET

It is important that your seed be fresh. Seed that has been on a shelf for many months can dry out and lose much of its nutritional value. If it becomes infested heavily with weevils or moth larvae, these pests can and will eat away the seed content. Mice as well as flies and other insects must be kept away from the seed, as they carry diseases which can infect your birds.

We recommend keeping seed in moisture-proof, covered containers. If you only have one bird or two, you can easily keep the seed in jars in the refrigerator. Once you start breeding, you may use so much seed that there will be no room in your refrigerator for both your food and the bird food, in which case we suggest keeping the seed in a cool dry place. Moisture and humidity will cause seed to mildew and become rancid. Stale seed can make your birds quite ill.

There are three tests to determine the freshness of bird seeds.

1. *Taste Test:* Crack a seed or two and taste them. Fresh seeds have a sweet taste. You will recognize bad seed by its sour, peculiar taste.

2. *Sprout Test:* We soak our seed in water overnight and rinse it with fresh water once or twice a day for two or three days. Within that time, it will start to sprout. Fresh seed will yield approximately 90% sprouts. These sprouts, by the way, are very good for your birds.

3. *Oil Test:* Press a small seed with your thumb on a piece of paper. A really fresh seed will leave a small circle of oil on the paper.

During hot weather a webbing may appear in your seed, which may then develop a filmy look. This webbing is caused by moth larvae. Even the cleanest seed may have moth larvae and/or weevils. Unless the infestation is

Opposite: *A lovely silver male cockatiel. In order to breed healthy young cockatiels, it is imperative that one begin with the best birds one can find.*

Above: *These cockatiels have show faults which would prevent them from winning at an exhibition.* **Below:** *Undersides of the wings of a male (left) and a female (right).*

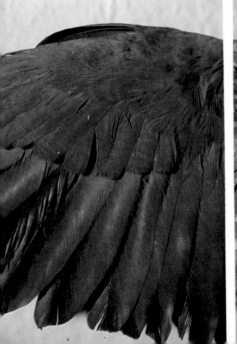

A group of newly hatched nestling cockatiels. Note the eyes and juvenile plumage on these babies.

really heavy, it will not harm the birds, although it will probably upset you. You can get rid of all the wildlife in your seeds by baking them in the oven for about 15 minutes. We suggest spreading the seed in a cake pan for baking.

A good seed mixture for cockatiels consists of corn, rice, millet, canary seed, oats and sunflower seeds with or without the shells. There are good commercial mixtures available already packaged. Many pet shops mix their own. Most of these are really good, but you can supplement them if you so desire.

Greens and Other Fresh Foods

There are several free greens you can probably find in your own backyard such as chicory and dandelion leaves. In addition, we feed watercress, lettuce, spinach, cabbage, celery, string beans and so on. We feed corn (either canned, frozen or fresh); the birds especially like dried corn cooked until it becomes soft. Apples and carrots are also enjoyable and nutritious. All fresh foods must be thoroughly washed before feeding.

Cuttlebone and Grit

Cuttlebone is the dried remains of part of the body of a marine animal very closely related to squids and octopuses. It is rich in calcium and other minerals. Many people think it is good for the birds' beaks to gnaw on the cuttlebone. Actually, it does nothing for the beak, but it does provide essential minerals for your birds. Especially at breeding time you will observe your birds ravenously attacking the cuttlebone. At this time they need an added supply of calcium for the formation of egg shells. For extra calcium, you can bake chicken egg shells in the oven for 20 to 30 minutes, then crush the shells and mix them in with the gravel or grit you provide for your birds. We add a little charcoal to the grit too; it sweetens the birds' stomachs and helps to keep them fit.

Vitamins

Though a balanced diet should provide adequate nutrition, just to be sure we use vitamins. There are several bird vitamins on the market, and pet shops carry many brands. We use one or two drops daily in the drinking water.

Water

It goes without saying that you should provide water for your birds at all times. Freshness is as important for water as it is for food.

MATING BEHAVIOR

The cock birds begin to show interest in breeding at an early age. From about six months of age and sometimes even earlier, they begin a distinctive mating call. It is a loud, repetitive, two-tone, two-syllable whistle that can

A cockatiel enjoying its cuttlebone. Cuttlebone comes from the cuttlefish; it is rich in calcium and other minerals which are an important part of the cockatiel diet.

go on for several minutes at a time. Females also call, but their call is more of a chirp and not as frequent or persistent. We suggest that you do not give your birds a nesting box or encourage breeding before they are at least ten months to a year old. This is to avoid frustration on your part, for it is likely that the eggs of very young birds will be clear or infertile. Also, a very young mother may quickly lose interest in sitting, feeding, etc.; she may even abandon the nest entirely.

Even if your birds are old enough, don't be discouraged if the first few matings produce clear eggs or only one or two fertile ones. Sometimes it takes them a while to get started, but once they do, cockatiels are prolific little birds.

When the birds are first introduced, the male will generally want to impress the female. He may spread his wings, whistle his mating call and show off any other whistles, words or tricks he has picked up along the way. The hen may be indifferent at first but should eventually respond to his insistent wooing.

Once a compatible relationship has been established, the pair will want to be together at all times and, if separated, will call loudly to one another and attempt to get back together. There will be a lot of kissing, cooing, grooming and feeding of each other, and cockatiels will demonstrate what appears to be genuine affection for their mates. It is especially appealing to watch the birds snuggle close, lower their heads and nuzzle each other tenderly.

The male will most likely be the first to explore the nesting box. Don't be surprised if the hen doesn't go anywhere near the box at first. The male will investigate, explore and literally move in. After a few days, he will encourage the female to come in and look around, and she will eventually settle in and stay in the box more and more each day. This is a good indication that eggs may soon follow. The male will continue to go in and out, feeding and courting his mate. The nesting box should be empty except for the concave wooden floor that comes with it. You may offer some cedar shavings if you like, but it is likely the birds will spend most of their time methodically throwing the shavings out of the box. One of our pairs, however, chipped away at the entrance to the nesting box as if they were trying to provide their own nesting material; they

seemed delighted when we gave them some ready-made chips to use. Once the birds are spending time in the nest and obviously courting, stay out of the nesting box. It doesn't need to be cleaned or disturbed at all, though you may take a daily peek to see if there are any eggs. Unlike canaries, who usually lay their eggs in the morning, cockatiels lay their eggs any time during the day. If there are no eggs in the morning, check again late in the afternoon.

During this time, cage cleanliness is more important than ever. The female will have larger, softer, odoriferous stools during the breeding period. Do not confuse this with diarrhea and do not give antibiotics or you may not have live chicks. You must keep the cage scrupulously clean. Be careful not to disturb the nesting box. If your cage has a removable drawer at the bottom to slide out and change cage papers, use it and leave the cage alone. Remember that a peaceful environment is more conducive to successful breeding than a noisy one. Cockatiels have been known to breed in the living room with the television blaring, in the kitchen with children running in and out— in fact, almost anywhere—but you will have more success if you place your cage in a quiet corner of the house where it will be relatively undisturbed. Of course, the more confusion the individual birds are accustomed to, the less it will bother them. You will have to use your own judgment.

As the birds get used to you and to their surroundings, they will uninhibitedly court and breed in your presence. Actual attempts at breeding may occur almost immediately after the birds are introduced, though many pairs take longer.

Cockatiel lovemaking is tender, but the male is dominant and there may be a few family quarrels. Don't be alarmed if he is aggressive. The birds may appear to be fighting occasionally and a few feathers may fly, but within a few minutes peace will be restored. There is no need to separate the pair unless one of them is really being abused by the other, a highly unlikely and unusual occurrence.

During breeding, the male mounts the female and actually stands on her back. He will swing

A pair of cockatiels engaged in grooming. This behavior almost always indicates that the birds are compatible for mating purposes.

his tail around and under the hen so that their vents meet, and he will appear almost folded in half. Generally, this will take place while the hen is standing on a perch and may continue for five to ten minutes. One wonders how the male maintains such an awkward position for so long. During breeding, the hen emits a continuous quiet chirp. It is so distinctive that you will learn to recognize it and will immediately know your birds are breeding. This may occur several times a day until the full clutch of eggs has been laid.

Incidentally, your male and female can co-exist in the same cage without breeding. Simply do not offer a nesting box and egg-laying will be discouraged. Should your female lay eggs anyhow (some hens do this even in the absence of a male), discard the eggs as they appear, and further laying should soon cease.

LAYING AND HATCHING THE EGGS

Once the hen starts laying eggs, she will produce one egg every other day until she has a clutch of four to seven eggs. The most important thing, once the eggs are laid, is that they be turned or rolled over each day. Your cockatiels will do this instinctively. However, if there is a broken egg or dried soil in the nest which can dry on the egg and glue it to the floor of the nesting box or to another egg, the eggs will not be movable; embryos in such eggs will die. Daily checking of the eggs to be sure they are free is, therefore, critical. Should one be stuck, gently loosen it with a soft cloth or cotton ball soaked in warm water. Be sure to dry the egg thoroughly to avoid chilling. Warmth is very important.

As the eggs are laid, you may carefully and very gently mark them with a soft, felt-tipped marking pen. Positively do not use a ball-point pen. It will puncture the eggs. We recommend that you leave the eggs alone, for they are easily dropped and broken, but you might feel better if you have identified each egg so that you know which ones you can expect to hatch first. As long as you are extremely careful, you can do no harm.

When the hen begins to occupy her nest daily, gently knock on the nesting box once every day to encourage her to come out for a while so you can have a look inside. It is important that she be used to moving easily in and out without becoming frightened of you, for should she get upset she may abandon her eggs or break them, either accidentally or intentionally. The calmer she is around you, the more likely she will be to accept you after the eggs are laid.

Your cockatiel hen may ignore her eggs for the first few days. There is no danger in this.

Incubation can start up to seven to nine days after the eggs are laid. Usually, the hen will start to sit by the time there are two or three eggs. If she isn't paying any attention to her obvious duties, leave her alone and wait a while. The mature hen will usually sit. If she is reluctant, the male will often insist that she sit on the eggs and will actually chase her into the nest. Many times, both parents will share sitting. The cock will sit during the day and the hen will sit at night with papa standing guard at the nest entrance. Many times, they will divide the eggs into two groups in the nesting box and sit inside together. If both birds happen to be out of the nest at the same time, don't worry that the eggs will cool. Cockatiels have a built-in clock that tells them when to get back to their nest. During the incubation period, you will be tapping on the box daily to coax the parents out so that you can check eggs and babies. When the

A pair of cockatiels in an outdoor aviary. Like most parrots, cockatiels will readily accept a hollow tree as a nesting site.

eggs are about seven days old, you can determine fertility by holding them up to a strong light. This is called candling. A fertile egg will look half dark or half full. If you do this, be sure you have identified the eggs, since the first ones will be hatching even before the later ones begin to look fertile. Just to be sure, don't discard any eggs at all until they are at least a month old.

The incubation period is approximately eighteen to twenty-one days. Normally, one egg will hatch every other day. If the female didn't start sitting on the eggs until there were two or three, those few might hatch at the same time or within a few hours of each other, but all the rest will hatch in the order in which they were laid. It is, therefore, possible to have a two-week-old chick and others of varying ages while the last eggs are still hatching.

GENERAL BREEDING

It is a good idea to cut your birds' claws before breeding. Cutting or filing will remove the sharp points which can break eggs or injure the tender skin of baby birds. If you are hesitant about cutting your birds' claws, get help from someone who is experienced and qualified to assist you. Usually your pet shop proprietor or your veterinarian will be glad to do this for you.

Some breeders pluck or cut the tail feathers of the hen to allow the cock easier access to the hen's vent for breeding. We haven't found this to be necessary.

The presence of a nesting box seems to act as a stimulant and encourages cockatiels to breed. It is possible, if the birds are mature, ready to breed and in excellent physical condition, that you will have eggs as early as seven days to two weeks after you set your birds up for breeding. Sometimes, even with active breeding, it can take longer. The average time is about four weeks after you observe your birds mating. Don't be impatient, though; you can't force or rush things, and you will have to have patience and confidence that your birds will eventually breed and lay eggs. If, however, nothing at all has happened after several months, it may be necessary to replace one or both birds and try again. This is the exception and happens very infrequently.

Before any cockatiel is bred, the owner must be sure that the bird is in excellent health. A sickly parent cannot possibly produce healthy offspring.

Raising the Chicks

Nothing is quite so ugly as a newly hatched cockatiel chick! Only a mother (or a breeder) could love the pink, baldish, disproportioned infants. Born wet, they soon dry and fluff up and are covered with pale yellow or white downy fuzz. They have very large heads with bulging closed eyes. As they peck their way out of their shells, empty shells will litter the nesting box. We make no attempt to remove them. Often the parents will remove the shells or push them off to one side. If, in a couple of weeks when all the chicks are hatched, shells still remain in the nest, you may safely remove and discard them.

Newly hatched chicks are totally helpless and will literally lie on the floor of the nesting box. However, they are quite capable of letting Mom and Dad know when they're hungry. You will soon hear a new sound—one that can best be described as a hiss—coming from the box.

At this point, be very sure there is ample food in the cage at all times. The fast-growing chicks require a surprising quantity of food. If they are not adequately supplied they will quickly die. Parents will be busy all day husking seed, eating and then feeding their young. They will store the food in their crops, pouches located in the throat directly under the beak. Partially digested food will be regurgitated and will come out as a creamy semi-liquid. This will be fed to the babies by both parents, and when you see the babies' food sacs (crops) full and plump, you can be assured they are being well fed.

This full appearance should be almost constant. Should the sac appear sunken and empty for more than a few hours, the baby may not be receiving enough food, and the job of feeding it will become partially or entirely yours. Don't rush to hand-feed, though. It is far better for both you and the chicks if the parents do their job. Try at this time to avoid too much obvious attention to the birds. There is a good chance that the protective parents will more readily concentrate on eating and feeding if they don't have to keep a watchful eye on you. If you're really concerned, observe from a distance so the birds are less aware of your presence.

A full diet including daily greens is important. The parents will use everything you provide to give the growing chicks a nourishing diet.

Cockatiel chicks appear to grow while you're watching them. Within a few days they will have doubled and tripled their size. Their eyes will open in about a week, and at the same time you

Opposite: *A pet cockatiel should have all the attention its owner can spare. Breeding cockatiels, however, should be spared too much interference, as the birds instinctively know what is best for their young.*

will notice the formation of small feather quills, especially in the crest, wing and tail areas.

At this point, when the babies are really beginning to look like birds, you may be eager to remove them from the nesting box for closer inspection and, of course, to show them off to the world. Carefully cup one at a time in both hands, and keep them out of the nest only briefly. Falls at this time will probably be fatal, so extreme caution in handling is imperative.

Before removing any chicks from the nest, be sure the parents are out. Slide a piece of cardboard over the nest opening so that they cannot get back in. You will have returned the chick to its nest before the parents are given access to the box. Never put your hand into the nesting box with the parents inside. You risk getting bitten; worse, the parents more than likely will get excited and may trample the babies and knock them around the box, possibly causing permanent injury. Babies are very thin-skinned and can easily be injured by the claws of a frightened parent.

It is a good idea to accustom the chicks to handling at this early age. Removal periods can be gradually extended as the chicks get older but should not exceed twenty minutes. After twenty minutes, babies get very tired or chilled and may miss a meal.

The chicks will huddle together in the nest for warmth. Mother will be sitting primarily on unhatched eggs and the youngest arrivals. Generally there will be adequate body heat generated within the nest for all of the birds to be comfortably warm. Chicks will continue to grow quickly and feather out rapidly. By the time they are two weeks old, they will start to look like their parents, but they will still be quite helpless. Their colors are obvious by this time, and you will see the beginnings of facial markings.

By three to three-and-a-half weeks, they begin to emerge from the nest at the insistence of their parents. They may sit at the entrance of the nest for a while, trying to summon the courage to move out. After a few days of apparent indecision, they are out! They may return to the nest off and on until they become totally comfortable in their bright new world.

Once the chicks are out of the nest, a good father will totally feed them while continuing to assist with the inside feedings of younger babies. He may even feed the hen, who may prefer to spend as much time as possible in the box with the younger chicks. This is the most strenuous time for the parent birds. Feeding an entire clutch is difficult and constant work, and your birds may appear to be in motion all day long.

The chicks move slowly and tentatively. Their footing is unsure, so they may have a few falls, but after a few days of practice they will move with confidence and ease.

Beaks of young birds are somewhat soft and will harden slowly. The parents will assist in feeding until the babies are able to eat and crack seeds by themselves. Their beaks will be hard enough to do this by about four weeks, at which time they are becoming independent and self-sufficient.

It is a good idea to make it easier for young birds to feed themselves by providing a mash for them. At about three weeks, we prepare mash using a mixture of cooked corn, high protein baby cereal and wheat germ. We never add eggs to a mixture that we put into the cage with adult birds. Although a little can't hurt, too

Although seed is an essential part of the cockatiel diet, young birds are not capable of cracking the shells until they are several weeks old. The parent birds will know when their chicks are old enough to handle seed.

much egg could cause albumen poisoning and death. Since eggs are not necessary for good nutrition, we prefer to take no risks. Using the ingredients in equal quantities, mix small amounts often so the mash can always be offered absolutely fresh about twice a day. Rancid food will kill young birds. We cannot overemphasize the importance of freshness.

By this time, the nesting box is a mess. Younger chicks may be soiled by the droppings of older chicks, and the box may have a very offensive odor. When the parents are out, cover the entrance and remove the nesting box. Place the chicks in a small basket or shoe-box lined with soft towels and quickly scrape and clean out the nesting box or replace it with a fresh new one. If the babies are heavily soiled, gently remove encrusted soil with warm water on a cotton ball. Do not soak the chicks, be careful not to damage their delicate skin, do not chill them—and be very careful not to drop them. We prefer to work over a table

Cockatiels in an outdoor aviary may limit their breeding season to the warmer months of the year.

covered with a thick layer of toweling so that if they do fall, they fall onto a soft cushion. As quickly as possible, get the chicks back into the clean nesting box, replace the box, open the door and allow the parents in to inspect their fresh clean brood.

Soon all of the chicks will have emerged from the nest. Don't separate them from their parents until you are absolutely sure they are eating and drinking properly on their own. This will take about five or six weeks from the time they are hatched.

Young birds will need to exercise. They will stretch their wings and be quite active in the cage. To avoid overcrowding, remove individual youngsters as they become ready. This is an excellent time for finger-training and taming. We advise you not to clip their wings until they are several months old. It is important for them to learn how to fly and to have exercise.

By the time they are eight weeks old, they will be ready to go to their new homes. You will probably have people waiting in line to take them, for individually raised birds that have been handled from a very young age make wonderful pets. If, however, you are planning to keep them, you will need a roomy flight cage so that they are not cramped for space.

It is not uncommon for the adult birds to resume mating while they are still weaning their first clutch. If you want to raise another brood immediately, leave the nesting box in place and the whole cycle will begin again. Two or even three clutches in succession are permissible if you want them. More than that will wear out your birds. After the second or third, remove the nesting box and give the birds a good rest for at least three to six months.

Possible Problem Areas

On the preceding pages we have described the usual sequence of events leading up to the successful completion of a breeding cycle. Providing all conditions are right, your cockatiels will breed easily and you will thoroughly enjoy the experience. Incidentally, there are variations in behavior that are perfectly normal. One of the pairs we set up for breeding when we began writing this book is a good example. Having not read the book, the young male did not know he was supposed to be the aggressor, so he didn't bother with the traditional mating call; he simply exhibited his acquired wolf-whistle at every opportunity and to every passer-by, including his mate. The hen, on the other hand, did everything but send the cock a written invitation to breed. She whistled, she called, she spread her wings and raised her tail feathers; she backed up against him and practically pushed him off his perch in her attempts to get underneath him. Eventually he caught on and performed as expected. Neither one of them got anywhere near the nesting box until they were ready to become full-time residents. This was the same pair that wanted wood chips in their nesting box so badly that they were chipping away at the box themselves until we offered cedar shavings, which they happily accepted. You must be prepared to discover for yourself some of the habits and individual peculiarities of your own cockatiels.

At the same time, you must be aware that there can be problems and in that event, though they are not frequent, you should be prepared to recognize and handle them as they arise. A quick but thorough visual check every day or even several times a day during breeding and nesting will enable you to assess your birds' well-being. They should be checked from head to tail. Any irregularity such as dull or watery eyes, beak encrustations or disorders, excess scratching, feather-plucking, broken or bleeding feathers or claws, diarrhea, etc., can be spotted early and treated before what might be only a small problem becomes a big one.

Should your birds develop a problem, there are several things you can do.

FAILURE TO LAY EGGS

If active breeding has taken place and no eggs have been laid after three to four months, there is little question as to who is at fault. Most likely your hen is unable to lay and should be replaced. If the hen produces eggs that are consistently clear, the cock should be suspected of sterility (or

Opposite: *A healthy cockatiel should have no trouble breeding healthy chicks. The owner must, however, be on the lookout for any problems that may arise.*

immaturity) and be replaced for immediate breeding.

FAILURE TO BREED

If there have been no eggs or observable courting behavior two to three months after setting up your birds it is natural that you will feel discouraged. Many factors can influence breeding behavior, and sometimes something as simple as moving the cage to a different location in your house may be all that's necessary. The birds might simply be immature or not in top physical condition. Any illness, sore feet, colds, mite infestation, etc., can be a deterrent to successful breeding. Though the majority of cockatiels will readily accept a mate of your choice, there may be a very few who prefer natural selection. Unless you have a colony of cockatiels, you cannot possibly provide your birds with the opportunity to select their own mates.

Once you have determined that failure to breed is not being caused by immaturity or poor health, the best thing to do (if your finances allow) is to buy another pair. Since cockatiels are usually so easy to breed, it is highly unlikely your second pair will not produce for you. If, however, you are the one in a million to whom this happens, you will have four birds and you can switch mates and try again.

If you cannot afford a new pair

or if you really want only one pair and if your dealer will cooperate, perhaps you can exchange one or both birds for a second try. Should you have two pairs of cockatiels set up for breeding at the same time, place a partition between their cages so that they can't see each other. This will avoid jealousy and distraction in general.

EGG-BINDING

When a hen is unable to pass an egg through her vent, she is egg-bound. This can occur at any stage of egg-laying, so successful passing of the first egg is no assurance that the others will pass easily, and your hen should be carefully and frequently observed during the laying period. If she is egg-bound, she will generally sit at the bottom of the cage, puffed up and shivering. We have seen birds literally in agony, hanging from the sides of their cages and thumping their bodies against the cage sides in an attempt to pass their eggs.

Prevention is much easier than the cure. The addition of a few drops of wheat germ oil or cod liver oil to the daily seed provides a natural lubricant as well as added nutrition. If, in spite of your precautions, egg-binding occurs, immediate action is essential. If the egg has not been expelled or removed within twenty-four hours, the hen is likely to die.

If your hen is egg-bound, heat

A pair of young gray cockatiels. Many breeding problems can be avoided if the owner takes care not to breed the birds at too early an age.

some water and fill a small pot or bowl so that the steam rises. Warm a little mineral oil, olive oil or any other edible oil you have in the house, drop one or two drops directly into the bottom of the bird's beak with an eye-dropper, and let her swallow. Do not attempt to push the dropper into the back of the beak. Any attempt to push the oil down her throat may cause your bird to strangle.

Turn your bird over and insert the tip of the eye-dropper into the bulging vent, being very careful not to puncture the egg. Administer one or two drops of oil into the vent.

Holding the bird with the vent area exposed, position her over the bowl of hot water so that the steam heats and moistens the impacted egg. Be sure the bird's feet are not hanging down and thus in danger of being scalded by the hot water. After the bird has been held over the steam for several minutes, it is preferable to put her into a separate cage, but since you probably have only one cage at this point, put her back with the male. Provide extra warmth, either by hanging an electric bulb over the cage or by placing a heating pad underneath it. Following this treatment, the egg should pass within twenty minutes to one hour. Place the egg into the nesting box. The hen may or may not nest and may or may not have the same problem with subsequent eggs. If she does, repeat the procedure as many times as necessary.

If the egg has not been passed after one hour, check with your veterinarian or a bird expert, for the egg will have to be broken and removed. Although this can be delicately done with a pair of tweezers, we urge you to have it done by someone with experience.

A hen who has problems of this nature should not be bred again, nor should she be encouraged in any way to lay more eggs.

LAYING EGGS OUTSIDE THE NEST

If a nesting box has been provided, it is safe to assume that an egg laid on the floor of the cage has been laid there by accident. Pick it up and place it in the nest. It is highly unusual for a hen to refuse to enter the nesting box. In the rare instance that she insists on laying her eggs on the floor of the cage, you will have to take your chances and let her sit outside the nesting box. Cleaning the cage will be difficult if not impossible, and raising the clutch successfully is unlikely.

INCUBATING THE EGGS

Should your birds refuse to sit on their eggs, it may be necessary for you to incubate them yourself. Fertile eggs need not be incubated up to about seven days after they are laid. However, once the hen starts sitting on them, incubation must be uninterrupted. If your birds will not sit on their eggs, you will probably want to attempt to incubate them yourself and raise the clutch without their assistance.

In other words, if your cockatiels sit on their eggs one or two days and then stop, you must immediately take over the job of turning the eggs and keeping them warm or the chicks will not

Although hand-reared birds make very tame pets, one should, if at all possible, allow the parent birds to raise their chicks. The success rate is much higher with naturally raised cockatiels.

develop. They will die. However, if your birds have not started sitting at all and are simply laying eggs as expected, you may safely wait up to a week from the time the first egg is laid before assuming they are not going to sit at all.

Attempting to incubate eggs requires almost total commitment. We urge that you do it only as a last resort.

There are several commercial incubators available. The best ones are expensive and hard to find. They turn the eggs automatically and therefore make your job much easier. Less expensive models are more easily obtained and will work just as well, but they require much more manual assistance.

Eggs must be turned at least two times within every twenty-four hour period from the day they are laid. However, it is best to accumulate three or four eggs before putting them into the incubator. If more eggs are laid, again permit three to four to accumulate and then put them into the incubator too. It is a good idea to mark these eggs with a felt-tipped pen so that you know which are older. Starting them in groups, rather than individually, will allow the chicks to hatch more or less at the same time and will make your job of hand-raising them much easier.

Before using your incubator, test the accuracy of the temperature settings. Proper temperature can be the difference between life and death for the chicks. Do not place eggs into a hot incubator. Heat must be raised gradually. Start incubation at approximately 90° F. and slowly move the setting up until the temperature is 101 F. by the end of the first day. On the second day, gradually increase the temperature to 102° F. and leave it at this temperature until the eggs are hatched.

Every day, spray the eggs with a very fine mist of lukewarm water. If the hen were sitting naturally, moisture from her body would keep the eggshells from drying out. The eggs must be turned over completely twice a day. Mark either the top or bottom of each egg with a felt-tipped marker so that you will know which side should be up and which side should be down. Some people turn eggs end over end. Some rotate them side to side. Actually, it doesn't matter so long as there is the proper movement daily to permit normal development of the chick embryos.

After the eggs reach the age of seven days, candling them (holding them up to a strong light to determine fertility) is a good idea. We never discard eggs until they are in the incubator for at least twenty-one days, but it is good to have an idea whether or not they have been fertilized and are growing. Generally, eighteen days is the incubation period for cockatiels. You will see a small hole, probably near the center of

the egg, and gradually it will become larger as the chick attempts to peck its way into the world. This is an exhausting job for a new baby and may take a few hours. Chicks will alternate periods of work and periods of rest. Remember that their beaks are just hard enough to break through the egg but much softer than they will be in a few weeks. Normally, cockatiel chicks will hatch without assistance. If you are impatient, though, or if you think the chick will really wear itself out, you may very carefully assist it. Newly hatched cockatiels have extremely tender, thin skin, so caution must be exercised to avoid injuring them if you are peeling away their shells.

Once they are out, they will be damp and downy. It is best to leave them in the incubator for a few hours until they are dry, fluffy and obviously doing well. Be sure, however, that there is an air supply in the incubator. Once they are hatched, the chicks need to breathe air.

A few days before you expect your eggs to hatch, prepare a small- to medium-sized box in which to raise the chicks. Arrange to have a 40-watt electric bulb over the box to provide heat and a heating pad underneath the box. Temperature inside the box must be maintained at about 80 to 90° F.

A cockatiel that is hand-tame will fetch a high price in the pet market.

Hand-rearing the Chicks

Examine the chicks daily. You cannot assume their parents are caring for them gently or competently. If, during your daily examination, you see any discoloration that looks like a bruise, more than likely the chick has been bitten by one of its parents. There may or may not be a reason for this. In some cases, birds and other animals seem instinctively to know whether their offspring are weak or deformed, and they take steps to eliminate inferior progeny. However, we have no way of knowing whether there is a legitimate reason for abuse or whether our birds are just poor parents. This situation is the exception, not the rule, and cockatiels are usually superb parents. There are many theories to explain abuse or neglect by so-called lower animals. However, our main concern at this point is to try to save the chicks, those that are being intentionally or accidentally hurt and those who may just be too small and too weak to survive on their own.

Sometimes, once the chicks begin to grow their feathers, their parents will pluck them out. At any stage along the way, parental abuse of any kind is adequate reason to remove the chicks and hand-rear them.

It is probably wise to remove them all, but if you wish only to remove the bruised or weak chicks and leave the ones who are apparently thriving, watch them especially carefully, since parents with a tendency to hurt their young are likely to repeat their injurious behavior.

If one or more chicks seem to be suffering from failure to thrive despite excellent care by their parents, remove and hand-rear them just as if you had hatched them in an incubator.

HAND-REARING

Cockatiel chicks can survive for the first twelve hours after hatching without being fed. After that, they will rapidly become dehydrated and die if they are not fed adequately and often.

There are many different formulas and many theories about the nutritional needs of baby birds. We treat our cockatiels as we treat our own babies and introduce new foods gradually until the birds can tolerate a full diet. For the first few days, we feed the following formula:

¼ cup high-protein baby cereal
¼ cup bread crumbs
½ hard boiled egg
¼ cup natural wheat germ
a few drops of milk

We mix all the ingredients together and puree them in an electric blender until the mixture is the consistency of a thick liquid.

Opposite: *Hand-rearing a healthy cockatiel takes a lot of work and patience, but it can be well worth the trouble if one is saving the life of a healthy but neglected bird.*

Previously, we mentioned albumen poisoning. So that you aren't confused, you should know that feeding hens are most susceptible to albumen poisoning because they are going from chick to chick and ingesting large quantities of food for an extended period of time. When we hand-feed cockatiel chicks, we can control the amount of egg we feed, so the birds are not in · danger. Rather, they benefit from the excellent nutrients in the eggs.

FEEDING

Prepare your work area first. We work on a table covered with a thick layer of toweling. This protects the chicks against injuries and fatal falls. Though we try very hard to hold onto them, they sometimes slip out of our hands. Have at hand a small bowl of warm water, an eye-dropper, a soft clean cloth, cotton, swabs and a small dish of prepared formula. We remove the formula from the refrigerator and put a tablespoon or two into a small glass. Place the glass into a dish of hot water. By the time the water cools, the formula will be warm enough to feed. Check the temperature on your wrist just as you would to test a baby's bottle. It should feel warm but not too hot.

Before you handle the infant chicks, warm your hands by holding them under hot water for a few minutes. The body temperature of birds is higher than ours, and chilling can be fatal to baby birds.

Sit at the table and support your arm by leaning your elbow against the table. Feed one chick at a time, leaving the others in the brooder to keep warm. Hold the chick in your hand with its back against your palm. Tilt your hand so that the chick is leaning slightly backward with its beak facing you. Fill the dropper with formula and wipe excess food off the sides of the dropper with the soft cloth. This is important, as it will help to keep the chick clean during feeding and will make your work easier. Insert the eyedropper into the beak, over the tongue. Squeeze the dropper and slowly feed small amounts of formula. You will see the food going right down the bird's throat into the crop. The chicks don't even appear to be swallowing; the food just slides down. As you feed, the crop will fill out. Don't over-feed, but give enough food to fill the crop so that it has a plump, full appearance. For the first day or two, this will be accomplished with a very small quantity of food, perhaps only half a dropperful.

When the crop looks full, you are finished feeding. With the cloth and warm water, clean the chick's beak, face and any other area that has food on it. Wipe out the inside of the beak with a cotton swab moistened with warm water. Food can dry and cake in the mouth,

A wild-colored cockatiel hen. The hen is easily distinguished from the cock by the yellow barring on the underside of the tail.

causing sore mouths, inability to feed and other problems. It can also become rancid if left in the beak and can cause upset stomachs. Feed each chick individually in the same manner until they have all been fed. In two to three hours, you will have to begin again. We give the first feeding of the day at about 6 a.m. and the last one before we go to bed, about 11 or 12 p.m. There is no need to feed through the night.

The unused food should be refrigerated. It will thicken when it's cold, but you can thin it by adding a little water.

About the fourth day, add to the original formula:

½ teaspoon wheat germ oil
½ teaspoon brewer's yeast
one or two drops of vitamins
At a week to ten days, add:
½ carrot
3 to 4 tablespoons of shelled
   sunflower seed or
2 to 3 tablespoons of peanut
   butter
1 tablespoon of honey

Continue to puree these ingredients in a blender and feed in the same manner as you did the first few days. Let the crop be the indicator of how much and how often to feed. As the birds get older, they will eat larger quantities at longer intervals. The crop should never be sunken and empty-looking. If it is, feed immediately!

By the time the chicks are ten days old, you may offer the food on a teaspoon. If you do, just mix all the ingredients by hand. It is not necessary to puree them in the blender unless you use the eye-dropper. It takes much longer to have baby birds feeding from a spoon. Unless you have a lot of time and patience, we suggest you use the puree and the eye-dropper until the birds are about two weeks old.

When the chicks are two to three weeks old, they have feathers and can survive at room temperature. Remove the heating pad from under their box. At this stage, they are strong enough to stand on their feet and support their body weight. They recognize you as their mother and will call you loudly with a hissing sound when they are hungry.

We use a small box for feeding. Prepare a dish of the formula and do not put it in the blender. Always warm it before feeding. Place the dish in the small box and put all the chicks of the same age into the box. Encourage them to eat with the spoon or by putting the food up to their mouths. They will learn quickly. If they are hungry when you attempt to teach them to eat by themselves, they will learn more quickly.

Provide fresh water for them at this stage, but be careful to use a container that they can't spill. They can be chilled easily if they are sitting or standing in spilled water.

After three weeks, you can introduce the chicks to bird seed. With a rolling pin, crack (but don't crush) smaller seeds. You can use a general parakeet mixture. Put a small dish of seed into the feeding box along with the dish of mash. The chicks will gradually begin to eat the seed. Don't stop feeding the mash, though, until you are sure the chicks are able to eat sufficient seed to fill them up.

At three to four weeks, parents

or other adult cockatiels may accept the babies and teach them to eat seed. Again, they can do a better job than you can do, so let them teach the babies if they'll do it.

Introduce babies into the cage one at a time, being careful to watch out for feather-plucking or abuse of any kind. If they are accepted by the adult birds, continue to provide cracked seed and mash for a while until you are sure the chicks can independently crack seeds and eat a full diet. This should be accomplished by the time they are six weeks old.

We eliminate egg from the mash if we put chicks in with adults. In an attempt to feed all the chicks, the adults may ingest too much egg.

Hand-reared babies can be put into a cage without adults by the time they are three to four weeks old. You may have to teach them to stand on the perches and show them where the food and water are, but they are rapid learners and should do very well on their own. They will respond to gentle handling. Especially if they have been completely hand-fed, they will regard you as their mother and will be affectionate and very tame.

Special treat foods for your cockatiel are available at your local pet shop. Such treats are especially helpful during training sessions.

COLDS

The first indications of a cold may be puffiness around the eyes, general listlessness, dull eyes, fluffed feathers and sneezing. Occasional sneezing by cockatiels and other birds is normal. It is their way of clearing their breathing passages. Don't confuse an occasional sneeze with a cold.

Once you have determined your cockatiel has a cold, the most important treatment is the provision of heat. In an effort not to disturb their normal sleep cycle, we prefer a heating pad under the cage instead of a light bulb over it. If the birds are not breeding and there are no chicks, you may safely use a light for heat.

Cold remedies are available at pet shops. These remedies will usually clear up mild colds. Follow the directions on the package for administration and dosage. If the cold progresses, antibiotics are highly recommended. Again, check with your veterinarian for a prescription and a proper dosage.

Because of their nasal structure, cockatiels have a difficult time draining their sinuses. Heavy caking of mucus on the beak over the nostrils must be removed or it will harbor infection and prevent the bird from recovering as quickly as it should. With warm water and a cotton ball, gently soften the accumulated encrustation and wipe it clean, being careful to avoid damaging sensitive membranes. After the nostril area is clean, put several drops of warm water into the nostrils with an eye-dropper. Empty the dropper, squeeze the bulb to form suction, place the tip over the bird's nostrils, and release the rubber bulb slowly to aspirate fluid and mucus from the nasal passages. We use the antibiotic solution for flushing and aspirating. This process may have to be repeated several times until your bird is breathing easily on its own.

These are drastic measures and are rarely necessary. We mention them only as a reference in the unlikely event you may need guidance. As a rule, cockatiels are hardy, healthy, strong and resistant to illness.

Keeping your birds well nourished, clean and out of drafts is the best way to aid them in maintaining their good health. We have no scientific evidence, but our experience leads us to believe that our birds can catch our colds. Should you have a cold, use precautions when handling your cockatiels, especially if they are breeding or caring for chicks.

Opposite: *A healthy cockatiel should have clear eyes and bright plumage.*

Certainly, breeding birds need not be kept in isolation, but since they are completely dependent upon us, we are obligated to use our common sense to keep them somewhat sheltered from unnecessary risks to their well-being.

FUNGAL INFECTIONS

If your bird has areas of skin irritation, it may have a fungal infection. Antibiotic ointment applied with a cotton-swab is an effective remedy. Use a fresh cotton swab when medicating separate spots, for you can spread the infection or re-infect an area that is clearing up by contamination with a soiled swab. Antibiotic ointments will have to be prescribed by your veterinarian.

BROKEN AND BLEEDING FEATHERS

When the birds become excited or frightened—and sometimes when they are introduced into a new cage—they flap their wings, bang against the cage sides or perches and break a feather or two. Most of the time, there is no danger in this. After all, we cut feathers and it is painless and harmless to the bird. Occasionally, though, the feather is broken close to the blood supply and will bleed when it is broken. If bleeding is excessive, you will have to intervene or the bird may bleed to death.

Using the towel method, grasp the bird and expose and extend the injured wing. Holding the wing in one hand, firmly grip the feather with the other hand and pull out the feather with a quick straight motion. You will need another person to help you by holding the wrapped bird; you need both hands free for this operation.

Bleeding will stop once the broken feather is out, and a new feather will start to grow back within a few weeks.

BLEEDING CLAWS

If a foot gets snagged in the cage and a claw is torn beyond the vein, you may see a blood-spattered cage that looks like a battlefield. Remove the bird and check all claws. Generally a styptic pencil applied to the bleeding point or a quick dip in peroxide will stop the bleeding. Continue to restrain the bird for several minutes to be sure of a good clot at the bleeding site. The bleeding may start all over again if the bird is released too soon and the bird is allowed to bang into something else, breaking the fresh blood clot.

FEATHER PLUCKING

Self-plucking is a subject of much controversy. There are dozens of theories as to its cause and cure. Birds that pluck their own feathers out have been accused of neurosis, boredom, poor nutrition, fungus, mites, an acquired taste for feathers, and so on. Using a process of elimination, try to determine the cause.

If your bird has mites, a good spraying with a bird insecticide should eliminate the problem and put an end to the plucking. If it is suffering from nutritional deficiencies, an improved diet and the addition of a few drops of oil to the daily seed should prevent skin dryness and irritation that might be the cause of pulling at the feathers.

Feather plucking is one of the most baffling bird problems, and there are no fool-proof or permanent cures. If the birds are plucking each other's feathers, remember that a certain amount is normal during mating sessions.

Plucking feathers, especially around the neck and crest areas of one's mate, is expected cockatiel behavior. However, if plucking is excessive, causing large bare areas and irritated patches, the offending bird must be separated from the others.

Plucking chicks' feathers by adult birds is considered parental abuse. In addition to preventing the babies from developing a warm, protective feather cover, it is easy to injure them, sometimes permanently, because they are so thin-skinned and delicate. If this occurs, remove the chicks immediately and either raise them by hand or give them to a willing and motherly adult cockatiel who will act as a foster parent and raise them for you.

Water is an essential part of your cockatiel's life. A water fountain such as this (available at your local pet shop) makes dispensing it easy and neat.

Breeding for Profit

At the present time, birds are the "in" pets. Everyone is buying them, and cockatiels are among the most popular birds. Bigger and more impressive than budgerigars, more trainable than canaries, smaller and less expensive than parrots, cockatiels are truly a salable commodity.

The keeping of breeding birds entails tremendous responsibility. You cannot simply "close the store" and take a vacation. You cannot leave, even for a weekend, without having made adequate provision for the care and supervision of your birds. Bird-breeding, then, becomes a seven-day-a-week, twenty-four hour-a-day job. It takes a certain amount of discipline to accept that and to maintain interest. If you get bored and sloppy, your birds and your business will quickly show the effects.

Because there are many problems such as epidemics of illness that can wipe out an entire aviary, which can occur with any livestock, we must urge you, if you want to be a commercial breeder, to start out small. Allow yourself ample time to encounter every problem and let your business grow with your experience. There is money to be made by breeding cockatiels, but you have to work at it and you must plan well in advance. If you set your business up the right way to begin with, you will never have to go through expensive remodeling and re-equipping. A lot of time and money are wasted by impetuous people who dash out without much forethought, buy everything in sight and realize later on that most of what they thought they had to have was the wrong equipment anyhow.

If we were to make recommendations to someone who wanted to breed cockatiels for profit, here are the steps we would suggest:

1. Spend some time in a cockatiel aviary. Cockatiels, like cockatoos, give off a powdery dust. You may be easily able to tolerate three or four cockatiels in your house, but you may be very allergic and sensitive to the dust and feathers of large numbers of these birds.

2. Decide how much money you want to make from your bird business. Is it to be extra spending money or do you expect to support yourself by breeding birds? In order to do this, you will have to check with pet stores in your area to see whether they will buy birds from you and to learn the wholesale price; when you get into larger numbers and you have

Opposite: *Breeding cockatiels for a profit requires that one begin with quality birds, feed a nutritious diet, and maintain clean surroundings.*

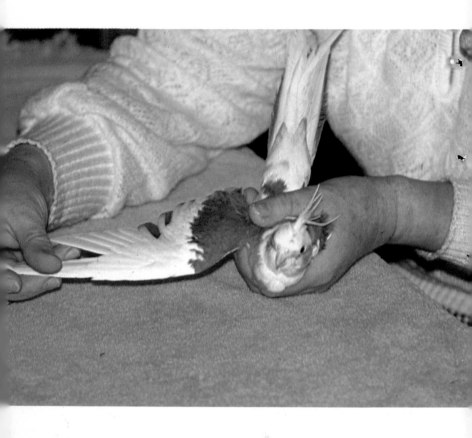

Prior to taming and training a cockatiel, it is advisable to clip one of the wings. **Above:** *The author has selected a male pied, and she spreads its wings.* **Opposite top:** *She locates the feathers to be cut.* **Opposite bottom:** *She then cuts them about half their total length. Before attempting this procedure, consult a veterinarian or an experienced breeder and let him demonstrate the proper method.*

to move birds, you will have to sell wholesale. We figure on an average of eight young birds a year from each breeding pair. You can see, then, that 100 pairs or two hundred birds will produce 800 young a year. Multiply 800 birds by the wholesale price and you will quickly estimate your income (your gross income anyway—the figure will, of course, be reduced by your expenditures).

3. In addition to your financial goals, the number of birds you keep will be largely dependent on the space you have available. We assume you will do this in your home. If you have to rent floor space or hire help to care for the birds, you will cut into your profits more than you can afford to do.

4. Normal gray birds are the easiest to breed for color. They have no eye problems or baldness problems like the whites, and their color is neither sex-linked nor recessive. All you do is help them to reproduce themselves. Unfortunately, they are also the least expensive and have the lowest wholesale value. If you breed the other colors, whites, pearlies, pieds, cinnamons, etc., you can command a higher price for your birds. You will have to exercise greater control of your breeders and, of course, you will have to pay more for your original breeding stock.

5. While you are counting the profits, don't forget your initial investment. It is expensive to set up properly. There are several ways you can do it. We prefer individual breeding cages for each pair. It allows us to know absolutely who is who, who produced what, when the birds need to be rested, and so on. In contrast to colony breeding, there is obviously no comparison. Therefore, we must again stress that you should determine your goals and proceed from there.

6. Consider the disadvantages of having many cockatiels. They make a lot of noise. Three or four chirp pleasantly. A hundred might drive you crazy. Consider the amount of constant work and constant surveillance. Consider the risks of illness. You will have to become an expert at observing even the slightest signs of illness, and you will have to become adept at handling the birds, administering antibiotics and other medications, etc. If something goes unnoticed, by the time it is obvious and you obtain professional help, you may have come close to losing your entire flock and your investment along with it.

7. These are all reasons for starting small and later expanding if you are successful and if you find you are enjoying your breeding activities. There are different ways to maximize your profits. We know one woman who sells her birds all tame and talking.

Headstudy of a pied male cockatiel.

They are very expensive and well worth the price. You can imagine the time it takes to produce these superb pets. She has to love them; certainly she can't produce too many, and we doubt that on an hourly basis she is making even the minimum wage.

If you're not discouraged yet, here are some other considerations. When you select an area of your house for your birds, it must be dry. A damp basement will assure certain disaster. Dampness causes arthritis, colds, rheumatism, mildew and odor. You must consider not only the birds but yourself as well. Your working conditions must be pleasant. You will be spending a lot of time with the birds. We suggest you paint and waterproof the walls and floor of your bird room. Bright daylight or artificial light that simulates daylight is essential; pet shops stock such lights. Cockatiels don't need a lot of heat. As a matter of fact, you can build your aviary outdoors.

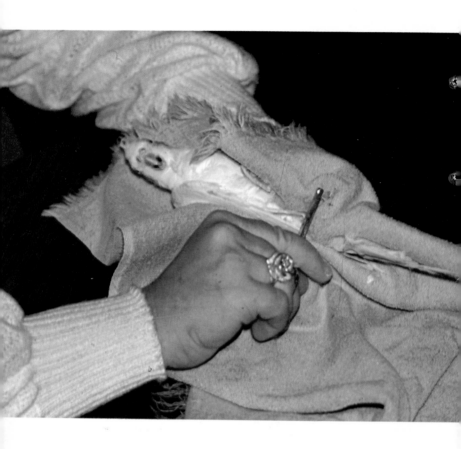

Above: *Before clipping your cockatiel's claws, be sure to have an experienced breeder or veterinarian show you the proper method.* **Opposite:** *There are many excellent dietary supplements for your cockatiel that are available at your local pet shop.*

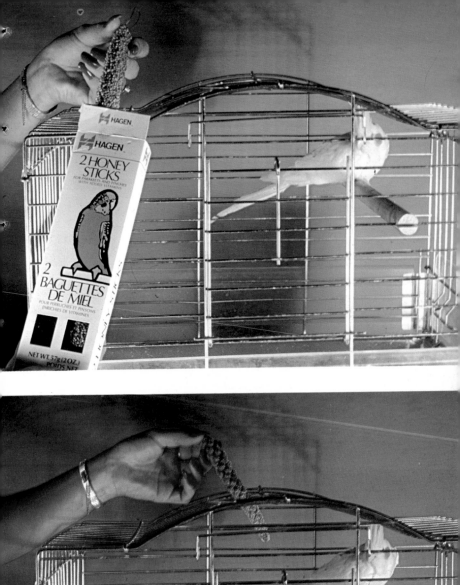

You will need adequate plumbing. Running hot and cold water is a necessity for watering the birds and cleaning. You will need storage areas for food, vitamins, medicines, extra nesting boxes, hospital cages, boxes in which to transport birds that have been sold, disinfectants, insecticides, etc.

It is a good idea, if you are keeping many birds, to buy your own seed in bulk. During your months of planning, check feed and grain distributors, line up pet shop bird buyers, look for the best deal you can get on cages and read everything you can find on building aviaries. Study plans, analyze how they would fit into your own physical set-up, visit other breeders and take the best from all of them. Basically, the two choices are colony breeding versus individual cage breeding. We have already covered the individual methods. There are a few additions, though, when you're doing it on a commercial scale.

1. We recommend spraying at least once a month with a good bird pesticide. Mites are more likely to find their way in somewhere with increased numbers of birds.

2. Be much more observant of birds that are slightly off. Diarrhea, colds, viruses, etc., can devastate your entire operation.

3. Be especially aware that fumes from backed-up chimneys, chemicals, stoves, etc., can kill. It is more serious to lose a breeding colony than it is to lose one bird. We are speaking strictly of economics here; we understand it is tragic to lose even one pet.

COLONY BREEDING

Colony breeding is by far the easiest way to breed if you want to do it for profit. We recommend using only normal gray or dark-eyed whites in colony breeding, though we are sure all colors have been successfully produced in colonies. Certainly in the wild all colors (to the extent that those colors exist—abnormally colored birds usually don't last long) breed with one another, but nature also produces mismarks, sterile birds, birds with bad eyesight, etc. In our controlled environments, we want to produce the maximum number of healthy, good-looking birds with the minimum number of problems. Six pairs are a good number for each colony. It is good to remember that the more room the birds have, the more likely it is they will breed freely and therefore be less likely to pick fights or feathers. In addition, the exercise they get flying back and forth will keep them in better physical condition. For six pairs of birds, we like 6 x 12′ flights, floor to ceiling. We use a layer of fine gravel on the floor, several inches thick. We rake it out to clean it,

A pair of cockatiels in a colony flight. Colony breeding is the easiest method for breeding a large number of birds. It does, however, cut down on the amount of control one has over breeding pairs.

and three or four times a year we clean it out completely, placing fresh gravel on the floor. In addition to the usual dowel stick perches, natural tree branches make wonderful perches and good chewing material. Before you use them, however, be sure they are thoroughly dry and free from insects. In addition to a large flight cage for each colony of breeders, you will need one for resting hens, one for resting males and one for young birds. You can see this is beginning to take up considerable space.

It is an absolute necessity to provide more nesting boxes than you have breeding pairs. For six pairs, we recommend at least nine nest boxes. It is amazing that cockatiels will fight over the most desirable home even though they seem all the same to us. Nesting

Above: *A pearlie female cockatiel sitting puffed up on her perch. This position could indicate that the bird is sick, or it could indicate (as in the case of this bird) that the cockatiel is simply preening.* **Opposite top:** *Some breeders use a small net to capture a cockatiel in its cage.* **Opposite bottom:** *Demonstration of how to hold a cockatiel over a bowl of steaming water in order to help the bird pass an egg.*

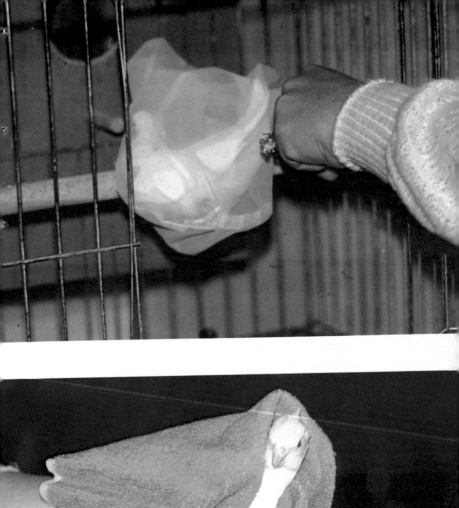

boxes can be attached to the flight walls or placed on shelves built into the flight. Having the nest boxes hung at alternating heights contributes to privacy and cuts down on fighting or simply curious investigation of what's going on next door.

You will never be sure which bird fathered which nest. Though they usually stay close to their own nest, it is not unheard of for a male to breed more than one hen. You must keep a watchful eye on the nests and the chicks to be sure all eggs and offspring are being adequately cared for. One advantage to colony breeding is the ease with which you can switch eggs around if necessary. You can give babies to foster parents if their own parents aren't feeding them well. You can remove feather-pluckers. You can have foster parents for any and all babies if for any reason their own parents are incapacitated.

THE BREEDING STOCK

For several reasons, you are better off buying young birds and letting them grow up together. First of all, they are much less expensive. Secondly, they will be compatible and friendly. It is sometimes difficult to throw twelve adults into a cage together. Cocks will fight over desirable hens, hens will fight just for the sake of fighting, and you may lose some feathers and sustain a few injuries. It can be done; we just find it easier to introduce youngsters to the colony.

You will not always know the sex of young birds, of course. After they mature and have lived together, you will see them pairing off; grooming each other, sitting together and showing obvious preferences. When this happens, put the pair into the breeding flight. Only when all the pairs have been determined and put together can the nest boxes be set up. Once that is done, keep all strange birds out of the room. It is important not to disrupt the harmony of a breeding colony. Being upset is contagious, and calm happy birds make better breeders.

Birds that have not paired off or extra hens or males can be sold as pets or kept as replacements if you have the space. We prefer to sell them and keep our numbers down to a minimum. We keep only the birds that are mated and producing. They have to earn their keep.

In order to assure the good health of the parents and the vigor, size and condition of the babies, we never permit our own birds to have more than two successive clutches of eggs. After they have produced two nests of babies, we separate the pairs and send them off to the male and female rest flights. There they live happily for at least four months,

A wild-colored gray male cockatiel. Gray cockatiels are considered the easiest to breed, but they fetch lower prices than do the fancier varieties.

after which they are returned to active breeding.

Cockatiels do not mate for life. You can feel free to pair birds that have not been paired before. With each new introduction, you must observe for awhile until compatibility is assured, but cockatiels are usually most agreeable and should not create a serious problem.

Allowing an average of four months from introduction of the pairs until the babies have fledged (left the nest) and a four-month rest period for the adults, you can produce two clutches per pair per year. We breed our birds from the time they are a year old until they are about six. Many breeders prefer to wait until the birds are two years old. They feel a more

Above: Using a heavy towel to protect yourself from being bitten, administer medicine with a plastic eye-dropper. It is a good idea to be sure that any medication given to your cockatiel has been approved by a veterinarian. **Opposite:** A demonstration of the proper way to hold a cockatiel. Note the head being held securely with three fingers so the bird cannot reach out and bite.

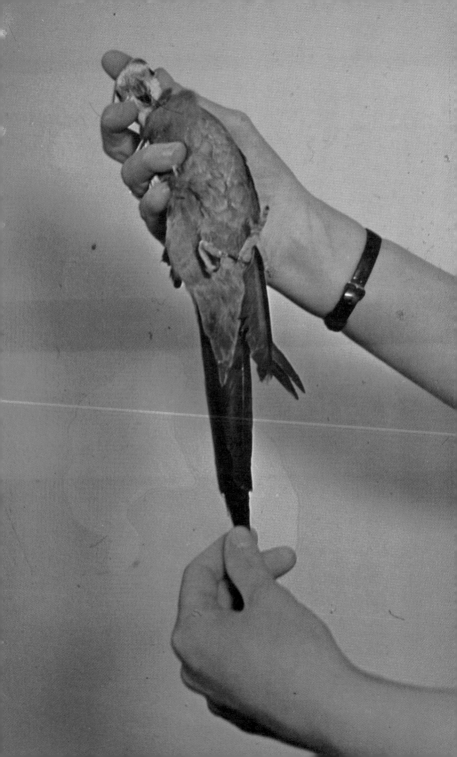

mature bird is stronger and can produce young of better size and strength. Actually, cockatiels have been known to breed as young as six months and as old as twelve years. Breeding too young cannot hurt a male cockatiel. The only problem is that he may not yet be able to fertilize eggs. By the time he is a year old, he is most likely mature enough to perform all his paternal duties. A very young hen may not lay eggs, she may lay infertile eggs, she may lay soft-shelled eggs, she may have a greater tendency to be egg-bound and she may be a poor mother. Rather than risk problems, we are content to wait a year or a little longer.

After six to eight years of breeding (even sooner if your birds are consistently producing two large clutches a year), we feel it is fair to retire them. Breeding, hatching and caring for young birds is exhausting work for parent birds. After a dozen nests have been produced, we feel they have earned a life of leisure— someplace else.

Many people sell these breeders as pets. Since cockatiels have a reasonable life expectancy, it is not unfair to sell a five- or six-year-old bird so long as you do not represent it to be very young. Once a bird is mature, it is hard to tell its age, so misrepresentation is easy. Ethically, it isn't the right thing to

do. Depending on the individual bird, its disposition may or may not allow the bird to be tamed and made into a loving pet. Usually, though, separated from other birds, cockatiels become dependent on their owners and develop a degree of tameness. If you are sentimental, you may want to keep retired birds yourself. This practice is certainly counter-productive if profit is your only goal, but if your operation isn't too big you can always find room for a few old favorites. Certainly you will always find good homes for them if you sell them very inexpensively or even give them away. Many people who simply can't afford a high-priced bird can give an excellent home to an older, less desirable cockatiel.

Our general advice about commercial breeding is to stay comparatively small and breed for whatever reasons give you pleasure and satisfaction. For some it is money. For some it is the thrill of helping to create life and to watch the process from infancy to maturity. Some people love to tame and train these adaptable little birds. There is nothing more satisfying than watching a young child discover the wonder of having a living bird sitting on his finger.

Many breeders get into genetics and color breeding. It is fun to try to develop new mutations or to perfect existing ones. A cockatiel

To maintain economy, keep only the birds which are healthy and will make good breeders.

generation is short enough for you to see results in a comparatively short time.

But if you're breeding birds only for money, you will have to be a little hard-hearted. Discard or destroy inferior birds, sickly birds, birds that don't produce. Your time is valuable, and you can't afford to waste it saving a lost cause the way you could if you were breeding only for pleasure. You must not compromise your standards in any way. Physical conditions must be ideal,

cleanliness is essential, fresh food is essential; scrupulous and daily care are the only things that can assure success. Those things, coupled with a little sales ability and much hard work, will go a long way towards making you a successful breeder of cockatiels for profit.

OUTDOOR AVIARIES

Cockatiels are hardy birds and can acclimate to living outdoors all year round providing you don't live in an especially cold region. If you

Above: *A breeding colony of cockatiels.* **Below:** *A pair of cockatiels enjoying momentary freedom.*

Above: *A pair of cockatiels engaged in mutual preening.* **Below:** *Mating may often follow a preening session.*

build your flights outdoors, there are advantages and disadvantages. Certainly cleaning is less of a problem. If your flights are big enough, a raking once a year is sufficient. You don't have to worry about electric lights—daylight is just fine. It is important that the flight cages are secure so that other animals cannot get in. Mice, rats and other rodents can spread disease and destroy eggs and baby birds. Larger animals will kill adult birds as well. The less wood you use in these outdoor flights, the better. Cockatiels chew wood severely, and the weather can rot the wood. We suggest constructing the outdoor flights so that they are covered. Canvas or lightweight aluminum is adequate. The covering is just to prevent the birds and seed from being drenched in a downpour. Cockatiels love a light rain, but being soaking wet for several days can be quite detrimental.

Outdoor aviaries limit the breeding season too. By being out of doors, birds will respond as they do in nature, breeding in the spring and resting during the colder months. There is also a risk of vandalism and theft and complaints from neighbors who may not take kindly to having a bird farm next door.

If you are out in the country and the climate is generally good, perhaps it might be a good idea to have your resting flights out of doors. We feel, however, that for better control of breeding birds and babies, and because we don't like to work outdoors in inclement weather, actual breeding and raising of chicks is better done indoors.

LEG BANDING

If you are breeding on a small scale, it is not necessary to band your birds. We don't recommend banding, because bands must be put on the birds while they are still in the nest; the parents, recognizing a foreign object on their offspring, may pick at it and inadvertently injure the chick's leg. If you do decide to use bands, you can camouflage the shiny bands by covering them with flesh-colored adhesive strips. Bands are made of aluminum or plastic and are open or closed. They are available in colors, so you can color code your birds as well as number and date them.

BIRD CLUBS

If you are going to continue breeding, you may enjoy belonging to an area bird club. Most local clubs are all-breed clubs; that is, their membership is not limited to cockatiel owners but includes owners of canaries, parakeets, finches, cockatoos, parrots, etc. Most of the people who are active in bird clubs are friendly and will give the beginner a warm welcome as well as often-needed advice. Making the acquaintance of other bird fanciers will also give you an added source for buying and selling your birds. If there are no clubs in your area, a small ad in your local paper will quickly mobilize the area bird lovers, and you can start your own group.

AMERICAN COCKATIEL SOCIETY

This is a comparatively new organization formed in 1977 to deal with cockatiels exclusively. Their purpose is to encourage an interest and understanding of the cockatiel as a pet, breeder and exhibition bird. The Society is eager to exchange ideas and keep in touch with members throughout the world. At present, the American Cockatiel Society has members in all 50 states and several foreign countries. They publish a news bulletin six times a year which has articles on care and nutrition, taming and training, genetics and other breeding

A pair of lutino cockatiels. Cockatiel breeding becomes more popular each year, and the quality of the color varieties continues to improve with planned breeding programs.

Above: *A gray male and a pearlie female sit close together. This is typical of a mating pair.* **Opposite top:** *A proud father with a newly hatched chick. Photo courtesy of Jeff Boyer, Lehighton, Pennsylvania.* **Opposite bottom:** *A very young lutino cockatiel being hand-tamed.*

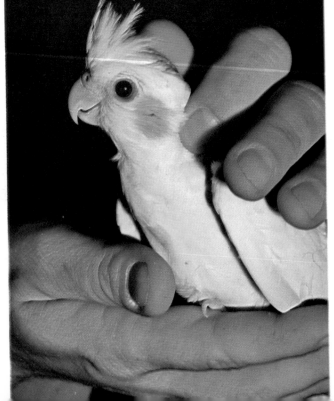

information; the bulletin also contains bird show information. You can obtain information about this society by subscribing to various bird publications.

KEEPING RECORDS

If you have enjoyed your first experience breeding cockatiels, you'll probably do it again and again and again. Before you know it, you'll be hooked, and if you have the time and space to devote to your new hobby, you can have the thrill of seeing the results of several generations of breeding.

Though your first few breedings may be just for fun, eventually you will want to improve upon your original stock and will selectively breed for size, color, temperament, talking ability or whatever else interests you particularly. You will be helped immensely by keeping detailed and accurate records. There are as many systems of record-keeping as there are breeders. We will tell you our system, and you can use it as a guide to develop one that works for you.

We keep a notebook with a page for each bird we own. On this page we record the bird's name (or an assigned number if it has no name), the date we acquired the bird and the person from whom we bought it, sex, color, markings and approximate hatching date (or age). Each time the bird is used for breeding, we

mark down which bird it was paired with, the date they were set up for breeding, the number of eggs laid and the number of chicks produced.

We keep another page for each brood of chicks, noting each chick's hatching date, color and sex, if known. We also record the final disposition of each chick (i.e. to whom sold or given, kept, died, etc.). We start a separate page for each chick we keep, just as we did for our original birds.

A three- or four-generation pedigree is a useful aid too. It will enable you to see your bird's background at a glance, and you will have a much better idea of what that bird will produce than you had when you bought your first cockatiel. You can put as much or as little information on a pedigree as you wish and all your record-keeping can be as simple or as involved as you like.

Genetics is a complicated science, but there are a few rules you will easily learn. You will discover dominant and recessive characteristics, sex-linked characteristics and much more. In his book *Encyclopedia of Cockatiels* (T.F.H. Publications), George Smith has written a marvelous chapter on cockatiel genetics. We recommend that you read it; you will find it interesting, informative and very helpful.

Record-keeping will help you identify your birds so you can

Cockatiels make popular pets, and the market for them is constantly expanding. Good food and proper care from the start will ensure healthy, happy birds.

linebreed if you want to and avoid inbreeding. Linebreeding is breeding back into the line; a hen to her grandfather, uncle or cousin, a cock to his grandmother, aunt, cousin, niece, etc.

Inbreeding is breeding brother to sister, mother to son or father to daughter. Though inbreeding can intensify good qualities, it can (and usually does) intensify poor qualities and weaknesses. You might produce birds with a trait you didn't even suspect you had in your line by the inadvertent pairing of two recessive genes. Inbreeding then, is something we categorically avoid.

SHORTCUTS

Any shortcuts you can find that save you time or work will maximize both your profits and your enjoyment of breeding cockatiels. Just a few we have discovered are as follows:

1. Use an automatic timer to turn lights on and off! You won't have to think about whether the birds have been put to bed. The lights will go off automatically at the time you specify. We always leave a very small night light on. If a bird leaves its nest at night, it can get confused and literally lost in the dark.

Steve Edelken, master kitemaker
and artist, created this long
"cockatiel" kite for the Rainbow
Kite Company of Venice, California.

Above: *Two views of a light yellow cockatiel.* Below: *Two views of a silver cockatiel.*

2. Use automatic feeders. You will find large seed and water containers in most pet stores that allow you to provide enough food and water for more than one day.

3. Especially if you are going to become a serious breeder, make every attempt to find other breeders in your area. Cooperating breeders can be extremely helpful to one another. They can trade secrets, advice, birds and bird-sitting services, and just a sympathetic, understanding fellow-breeder can be a tremendous comfort and help when you are discouraged, when you have a problem you've never had before or when you want a particular bird or birds you cannot manage to breed yourself. It's always nice to share your successes too. There is nothing like a person who's been through it himself to share your joys and sorrows.

4. It cannot be suggested strongly enough that you read everything you can find about cockatiels and talk to as many people as you can. Even though much of the information you acquire will be facts you already know, each individual or book is likely to give you one or two choice pearls of wisdom that make it all worthwhile.

5. We recommend that you keep a diary, at least as a beginner. Record what happened, what you did about it, what the results were. You will be surprised at how much you forget, and in a year or so your own diary will be a source of information. You will also be pleased to discover, after some experience, how much you've learned and how much you've been enriched by the experience of breeding cockatiels.

6. Your pet shop owner can be a big help. He has heard every story and probably seen every cockatiel problem imaginable. He is most likely familiar with the available literature and can recommend the best books, the best foods and the best local veterinarians experienced in bird care. Your pet dealer can be your ally and your friend and, of course, if you breed enough birds, he can be your customer as well as your supplier.

You have chosen a very popular bird to breed, one that makes a fine pet, a charming companion, an easy breeder and a quick seller—and one that has a definite potential to fulfill a variety of purposes for its owners. In the book *Parrots and Related Birds*, Henry Bates and Robert Busenbark state:

"If we were suddenly denied the pleasure of all our birds except one, we would unhesitatingly choose a Cockatiel to be that one pet . . best of all easily reared birds. No bird can be more highly recommended than a Cockatiel."

Index

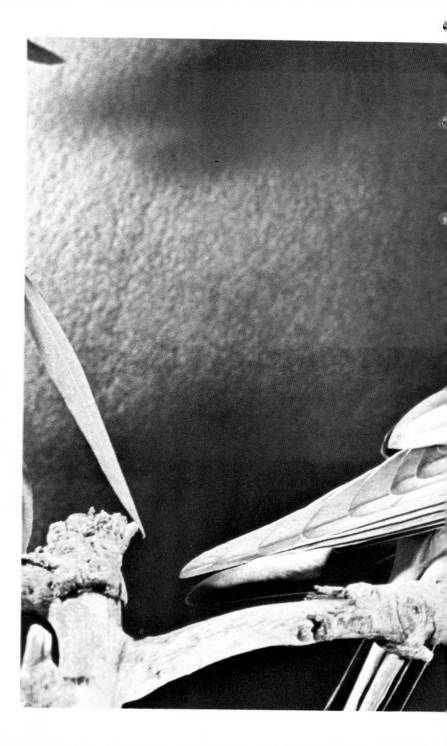

BREEDING COCKATIELS
KW-099